LET'S ROCK!

EXPLORING SEDIMENTARY ROCKS

MARIE ROGERS

PowerKiDS press
New York

Published in 2022 by The Rosen Publishing Group, Inc.
29 East 21st Street, New York, NY 10010

First Edition

Editor: Amanda Vink
Cover Designer: Alan Sliwinski
Interior Designer: Rachel Rising

Portions of this work were originally authored by Maria Nelson and published as *Earth's Minerals*.
All new material this edition authored by Marie Rogers.

Photo Credits: Cover kojihirano/Shutterstock.com; Cover, pp. 1, 3, 4, 5, 6, 7, 8, 10, 11, 12, 14, 15, 16, 18, 19, 20, 21, 22, 23, 24 (background) Alex Konon/Shutterstock.com; p. 4 Aleksandr Pobedimskiy/Shutterstock.com; p. 5 Bas van der Pluijm/Shutterstock.com; p. 7 Nasky/Shutterstock.com; p. 8 sonsart/Shutterstock.com; p. 9 NumZX/Shutterstock.com; p. 11 YuRi Photolife/Shutterstock.com; p. 12 Tom Grundy/Shutterstock.com; p.13 Harry Beugelink/Shutterstock.com; p. 14 Martina_L/Shutterstock.com; p. 15 Nickolay Vinokurov/Shutterstock.com; p. 16 Anelena/Shutterstock.com; p. 17 luisrsphoto/Shutterstock.com ; p.18 losmandarinas/Shutterstock.com; p. 19 Amit kg/Shutterstock.com; p. 20 Mega Pixel/Shutterstock.com; p. 21 WildDrone/Shutterstock.com; p. 22 Eugen Thome/Shutterstock.com.

Cataloging-in-Publication Data

Names: Rogers, Marie.
Title: Exploring sedimentary rocks / Marie Rogers.
Description: New York : PowerKids Press, 2022. | Series: Let's rock! | Includes glossary and index.
Identifiers: ISBN 9781725319257 (pbk.) | ISBN 9781725319271 (library bound) | ISBN 9781725319264 (6 pack)
Subjects: LCSH: Sedimentary rocks–Juvenile literature. | Rocks–Identification–Juvenile literature. | Geology–Juvenile literature.
Classification: LCC QE471.R5936 2022 | DDC 552.5–dc23

Manufactured in the United States of America

CPSIA Compliance Information: Batch #CWPK22. For further information contact Rosen Publishing, New York, New York at 1-800-237-9932.

CONTENTS

SEDIMENTARY ROCKS 4

WEATHERING AND EROSION 6

SORTING 8

LAYERS 10

CLASTIC ROCK 12

NONCLASTIC ROCK 14

DRIPPING 16

CLASSIFICATION 18

FOSSIL FUELS 20

A PICTURE OF HISTORY 22

GLOSSARY 23

INDEX 24

WEBSITES 24

SEDIMENTARY ROCKS

Sedimentary rock makes up less than 1 percent of Earth's total volume. However, because it's about 75 percent of Earth's land surface, it's a type of rock humans see a lot! Sedimentary rocks are found all over the world.

While other rocks commonly form under hot conditions, sedimentary rocks begin as sediment, or small pieces of sand, rock, minerals, and other matter. Sedimentary rocks form on or near Earth's surface. They tell us a lot about how Earth has changed over time. For example, if limestone is discovered on land, it's likely that at one time the area was under water.

LIMESTONE

ROCKING OUT

In addition to sedimentary rocks, there are igneous rocks and metamorphic rocks. All rocks move between points in the rock cycle, which shows how rocks change when exposed to different forces, such as pressure or heat.

Limestone is often made, in part, of the shells of underwater animals.

WEATHERING AND EROSION

The processes of weathering and erosion create sedimentary rocks. Both are caused by wind, water, and gravity.

Weathering is when forces work on a rock to wear it down. Over time, even the largest boulders break down. Chemical weathering is when something, such as water, causes a chemical change in the structure of a rock. It might make it softer. Then, it's easier for mechanical weathering, which is when something breaks down the **physical** structure of the rock. Oxygen and carbon dioxide can cause chemical weathering.

Erosion is the removal and **transport** of sediment worn off a rock. When energy from wind or water motion becomes too weak to carry it, sediment settles in a new location.

Sedimentary rocks form from pieces of other rocks. Weathering and erosion create sediment that becomes sedimentary rock. This is an important part of the rock cycle.

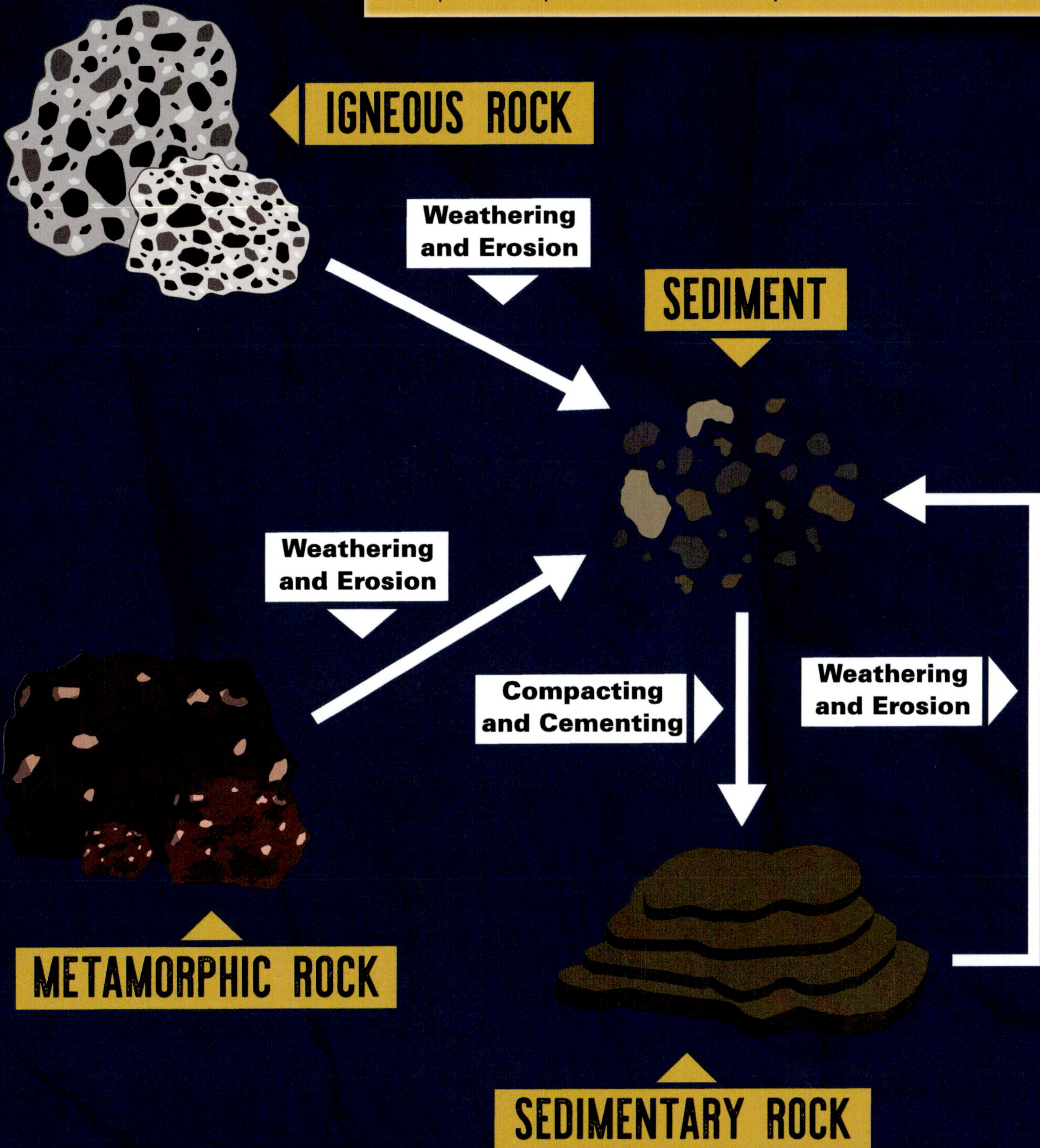

SORTING

As wind and water carry sediment, the many tiny pieces of rock bump and slide against each other. This process can make them smooth and round. Often, the rock **particles** will travel different distances depending on what size and **mineral** they are. This natural separation of sediment is called sorting. Well-sorted sediment has particles that are similar in size. Poorly sorted sediment has particles of many different sizes.

In time, particles settle into a new location. Other matter builds on top of the sediment and presses on it. Animals and humans may walk on it. Water can flow over it.

This sedimentary rock is poorly sorted. It's made of sediment of many sizes.

LAYERS

As sediment is buried deeper and deeper, the pressure against it increases. Lithification is the process by which sediment is subject to pressure, **compacts**, and turns into rock. Water mixed with minerals may flow into the sediment, filling open spaces. The sediment then changes to rock. This process is called **cementing**.

Because of the way sediment is **deposited**, sedimentary rock is often layered, which is called stratification. The oldest layers, or strata, are on the bottom, and the newest layers are at the top. Scientists "read" sedimentary rock and date strata to find out what happened millions of years ago.

Because of the high heat needed to form igneous and metamorphic rock, scientists don't usually find fossils there—but it can happen.

ROCKING OUT

Fossils are the traces of ancient life left in rock. A fossil forms in just the right conditions after an animal or plant is buried quickly and minerals replace or fill in the gaps. When the rock erodes, the fossil is exposed.

CLASTIC ROCK

Sedimentary rocks are split into two main groups: clastic rock and nonclastic rock.

Clastic sedimentary rocks are made up of pieces of preexisting rocks and minerals. These pieces, called clasts, are the result of mechanical weathering. Clastic sedimentary rock may also have pieces of shells, pebbles, and other objects compacted in it.

Shale and sandstone are two common types of clastic sedimentary rocks. Shale is made of sand-sized grains of minerals, and scientists **estimate** that shale makes up three-quarters of the sedimentary rock in Earth's crust. Sandstone is made of fine-grained particles, and it too can be found all over the world.

SHALE

People have used both shale and sandstone to build homes and other structures for centuries.

NONCLASTIC ROCK

Nonclastic sedimentary rocks are formed from chemical reactions. They often look and feel smoother than clastic rocks. Most are formed in the ocean. Rock salt forms when very salty water evaporates, or turns into vapor, and leaves the mineral halite behind. People use rock salt to keep highways free of ice during winter months.

Some nonclastic sedimentary rocks are made of organic matter. Coal, for instance, forms from plants and animals that died long, long ago and were buried under sediment. Chalk is a nonclastic sedimentary rock that forms deep in oceans. It is made from the calcite shells of microscopic sea creatures that settle to the ocean floor.

ROCK SALT

ROCKING OUT

When a lake dries up over many thousands of years, mineral deposits are often left behind. This is a form of precipitation, which is when rocks form from chemicals separated from water. These types of rocks are often called evaporites.

Located near Israel and Jordan, the Dead Sea is one of the saltiest bodies of water in the world. The lake's water levels are falling quickly because of human activity.

DRIPPING

The cave formations called stalagmites and stalactites are made of sedimentary rock formed by chemical means. These structures form when water makes its way into a cave after picking up calcium and carbonate ions from bedrock. It drips down through cracks. When the water evaporates, calcium carbonate is left behind. Over time, pointy shapes form. If it's on the ceiling, it's a stalactite. If it's on the floor of the cave, it's a stalagmite. Sometimes these grow together and form a column.

Usually these structures are found in limestone caves. Both terms come from the Greek word *stalassein*, which means "to drip."

CALCITE TAKEN FROM A STALACTITE

Many people explore caves in search of these astounding structures.

CLASSIFICATION

Sedimentary rocks are first **classified** by whether they are clastic or nonclastic. Then scientists can make further classifications.

Clastic sedimentary rocks are grouped by **texture**, or the size of the sediments that formed them. For example, siltstone is a clastic sedimentary rock made of mud, and its texture is very fine. Breccia is a clastic sedimentary rock made of gravel, and it has a course, or uneven, texture.

Nonclastic sedimentary rocks are also grouped by what they're made of. Limestone, a gray, soft rock, is made from calcite. Diatomite, a white, powdery rock, is made from microquartz.

BRECCIA

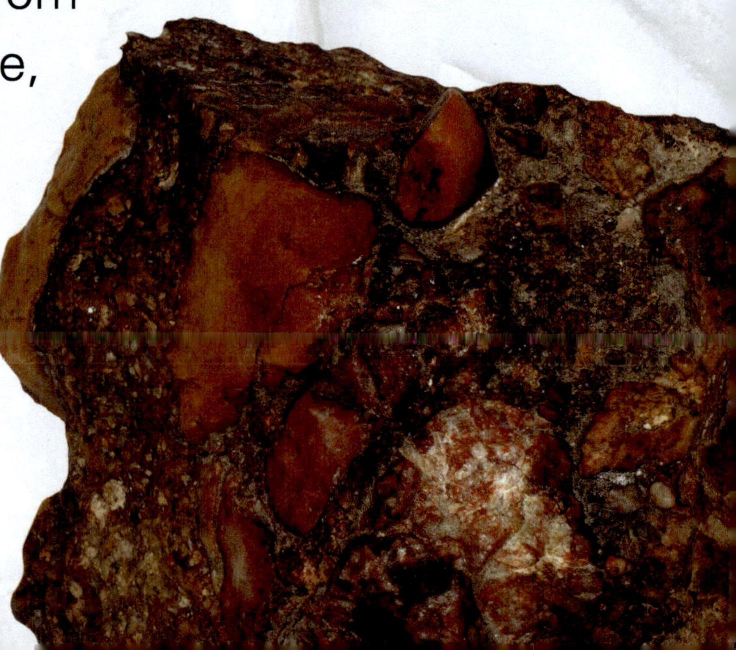

ROCKING OUT

Scientists can find out a lot about a rock by the way it breaks. That's because minerals form in particular ways. Cleavage is the way some minerals tend to break along a flat plane. Fracture is the way some minerals break when it's not along a plane.

Siltstone is often used to make cement. Because of its interesting appearance, people sometimes use breccia to make sculptures and gems.

SILTSTONE

FOSSIL FUELS

Sedimentary rock formation may produce important natural **resources** called fossil fuels. Fossil fuels come from the remains of long-dead plants and animals, and they can be used to make energy.

One kind of fossil fuel that comes from lithification is coal. It's an organic sedimentary rock that forms from plant and animal remains. There's a lot of coal, and it's cheap. In the past and today, coal is used to create power.

However, fossil fuels are a nonrenewable, or limited, resource because they take a very long time to form. Humans are trying to find other means of creating energy.

COAL

ROCKING OUT

Some people mine for coal as a job. Some people love the job, but it can be dangerous work. In the United States, coal mining is a shrinking industry.

Burning fossil fuels is costly for Earth. They give off **emissions** that are a main cause of climate change.

A PICTURE OF HISTORY

It's important to study sedimentary rocks because they tell us about Earth's history. They can tell us how a sea turned to a desert and how animals changed over time.

The same natural laws and processes that exist today also existed in the past. Geologists often look at land formations and fossils to see what happened in the past. Although the same processes aren't always at work all the time, this idea can help geologists paint a picture of Earth's timeline.

Sedimentary rocks are central to painting this picture because they're records of the past. What will you see next time you look at a sedimentary rock?

GLOSSARY

cement: To unite or make firm.

classify: To arrange into groups.

compact: To pack firmly together.

deposit: To put something down and leave it behind, or something that's been put down and left behind.

emission: Something sent out or given off.

estimate: To make a guess based on the information you have about the size, amount, etc., of something.

mineral: A naturally occurring solid substance that's not of plant or animal origin.

particle: A very small piece of matter.

physical: Relating to something solid or material.

reaction: A response to something.

resource: Something that can be used.

texture: The way something feels when you touch it.

transport: The process by which something's carried from one place to another.

INDEX

B
breccia, 18

C
calcium, 16
chalk, 14
chemical reactions, 14
chemical weathering, 6
clastic rock, 12, 18
cleavage, 19
coal, 14, 20, 21

D
Dead Sea, 15
diatomite, 18

E
erosion, 6, 7
evaporites, 15

F
fossil fuels, 20, 21
fossils, 10, 12, 22
fracture, 19

G
gravity, 6

H
halite, 14

I
igneous rocks, 5, 7, 10

L
limestone, 4, 5, 16, 18
lithification, 10, 20

M
mechanical weathering, 6, 12
metamorphic rocks, 5, 7, 10
minerals, 8, 10, 11, 12, 14, 15, 19

N
nonclastic rock, 12, 14, 18

O
organic sedimentary rock, 14, 20

P
precipitation, 15

R
rock cycle, 5, 7
rock salt, 14

S
sandstone, 12, 13
shale, 12, 13
siltstone, 18, 19
sorting, 8
stalactites, 16
stalagmites, 16
stratification, 10

W
water, 6, 8, 14
weathering, 6, 7, 12
wind, 6, 8

WEBSITES

Due to the changing nature of Internet links, PowerKids Press has developed an online list of websites related to the subject of this book. This site is updated regularly. Please use this link to access the list:
www.powerkidslinks.com/letsrock/sedimentary